09
––
1 10

ROARING RIDES

STOCK CARS

TRACY NELSON MAURER

Rourke

Publishing LLC

Vero Beach, Florida 32964

www.rourkepublishing.com

Project Assistance
Ed Newman, AMSOIL INC.

Also, the author extends appreciation to Mike Maurer, Chuck Abrams, and Kendall and Lois M. Nelson.

Photo Credits: Cover and pages 4, 14, 16 © Donald Miralle/ALLSPORT; Title page and page 11 © Jon Ferrey/Getty Images; page 9 © Brian Cleary/Getty Images; pages 10, 37 © James Squire/Getty Images; pages 18, 21, 23 © Darrell Ingham/Getty Images; pages 25, 40/41 © John Chiasson/Getty Images; page 29 © Rober Laberge/Getty Images; page 33 © DigitalGlobe.com/Getty Images; page 43 © Peter Carvelli/Getty Images; page 7 © Hulton/Archive/Sherman; page 34 © Jeff Gross/ALLSPORT

Title page: Dale Earnhardt Jr. driving his #8 car March, 2003

Editor: Frank Sloan

Cover and page design: Nicola Stratford

Notice: The publisher recognizes that some words, model names, and designations mentioned herein are the property of the trademark holder. We use them for identification purposes only. This is not an official publication.

Library of Congress Cataloging-in-Publication Data

Maurer, Tracy, 1965-
  Stock cars / Tracy Nelson Maurer.
    p. cm. -- (Roaring rides)
Summary: Discusses the history and current popularity of stock cars and their drivers, as well as the races in which they compete.
Includes bibliographical references and index.
  ISBN 1-58952-751-8 (hardcover)
  1. Automobiles, Racing--Juvenile literature. 2. Automobile racing--Juvenile literature. [1. Automobiles, Racing. 2. Automobile racing. 3. NASCAR (Association)] I. Title. II. Series: Maurer, Tracy, 1965-   Roaring rides.
  TL236.M356 2003
  629.228--dc21
                                                    2003010021

Printed in the USA

w/w

TABLE OF CONTENTS

CHAPTER ONE   NASCAR REVS UP 5

CHAPTER TWO   STOCK, BUT NOT 15

CHAPTER THREE   AIR POWER 27

CHAPTER FOUR   HEADED FOR VICTORY LANE 35

CHAPTER FIVE   LIFE ON THE ROAD..........................39

FURTHER READING 45

WEB SITES 45

GLOSSARY 46

INDEX 48

Fans of all ages flock to stock car races. Stock car racing is one of America's most popular sports.

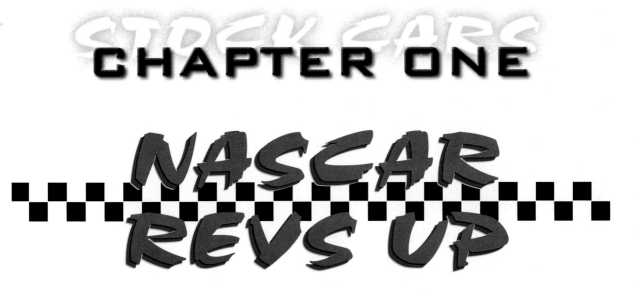

CHAPTER ONE

NASCAR REVS UP

American kids love to pretend it's race day. They "drive" red wagons and cardboard boxes, making sound effects for squealing tires and roaring engines.

Although adults usually skip the sound effects, they often play "racecar driver" like kids do. Adults imagine roaring around a track at 200 miles (321 km) per hour as they grind through freeway traffic. Maybe that's why stock car racing has become so popular—it's an easy sport for fans of all ages to understand.

MOONSHINE RUNS

Stock car racing traces its roots to the southeastern United States in the 1930s. Some people illegally brewed and sold liquor in the hilly forests there. They hired drivers to deliver the "moonshine" to nearby towns. Speeding along rutted and winding roads, the drivers often tried to outrun police along the way.

When moonshine runners had no jobs, they raced each other—illegally, at first. Soon, the races moved onto legal dirt tracks. But the "rules" changed with nearly every race.

THE FIRST WAVE

Legal racing continued farther south on Florida's beaches. The hard-packed sand tracks challenged drivers, especially when their cars took an unexpected dip in the ocean.

The shoreline excitement attracted small crowds. Bill France, Senior, who entered some of Florida's beach races, thought the audiences could grow much larger. He held his own race in 1938 at Daytona Beach. France made enough money to hold bigger and better races. He created the National Association for Stock Car Auto Racing (NASCAR) in 1948 to make racing rules, increase safety, and promote a better image for the sport.

In 1956, some teams hauled their race-ready stock cars to the tracks. Others drove their racers there.

MAKING CHAMPIONS

Like many other early racing organizations, the new NASCAR didn't have a way to name a true national champion—a hook for catching loyal fans.

In June 1949, Bill France, Sr., introduced NASCAR's Grand National series. He created a point system for drivers that would decide one national champion at the end of the season. France also limited the races to strictly stock models, cars anyone could buy from a local dealer's stock.

France made the rules and stuck to them—sometimes more strictly than the drivers liked. He believed his tight control was the only way for NASCAR to lead the most popular racing circuit. His plan worked. He served as president of NASCAR for 24 years and guided stock car racing's amazing growth.

ROARING FACT

Automobiles first started racing on the sand at Daytona Beach in 1903. The National Association for Stock Car Auto Racing (NASCAR) held its first race there on February 15, 1948.

Bill France, Jr., now leads the NASCAR program. NASCAR owes much of its success to the France family.

RACING'S BIGGEST AND BEST

After 55 years of operation, NASCAR reigns as the world's largest stock car racing organization. It runs more than 40 race tracks and holds about 300 professional races every year. NASCAR **sanctions** the NASCAR Regional Touring Series and the NASCAR Weekly Racing Series, plus three national series: Nextel Cup Series (starting in 2004), Busch Grand National Series, and Craftsman Truck Series.

By 2003, the Winston Cup Series topped NASCAR racing with the biggest prizes, the fastest cars, and the most fans. More than 60 million people—about half of them women—in over 100 countries watch the Cup races on television. A new sponsor, Nextel, promises to continue to support NASCAR racing well into the future.

PROFESSIONAL STOCK CAR FAST FACTS

GENERAL TOP SPEED:	200 miles (321 km) per hour
GENERAL TOP HORSEPOWER:	700 (450 HP with restrictor plate)
MAXIMUM HEIGHT:	51 inches (129.5 cm)
MAXIMUM WIDTH:	79 inches (200.1 cm)
MINIMUM WEIGHT:	3,400 pounds (1,542 kg) without driver

◀ *The Winston Cup Series became the major attraction in the NASCAR program. Nextel signed on as the new sponsor in 2003.*

CHECKING FOR CHEATERS

Under the leadership of Bill, Jr., the France family still holds a tight grip on NASCAR. The organization decides racetrack sizes, course miles, car numbers, how many drivers in a race, and who drives in which race. Some tracks have special rules, too. The official race rulebooks are available only to NASCAR members.

Racing teams *must* know the rules. Judges from NASCAR check to make sure all the cars meet the standards for size, shape, parts, and whatever else (without an official rulebook, nobody outside of NASCAR knows for sure!).

NASCAR can **disqualify** cheaters. The rules help to keep the cars equal, so a driver's skill—and a bit of luck—wins the race.

BEYOND NASCAR

Every warm-weather weekend, racetracks host thrilling stock car action that's not part of NASCAR. The American Speed Association (ASA), founded in 1968, focuses on short-track stock car racing.

Many top drivers come from the Automobile Racing Clubs of America (ARCA) circuit. John Marcum, a former employee of Bill France, Sr., created ARCA in 1953. Today ARCA sanctions more than 100 races every year. The ARCA Re/Max Series features cars similar to top NASCAR models, but ARCA runs on dirt or paved tracks.

The National Hot Rod Association, National Muscle Car Association, Indy Racing League, World of Outlaws, and CART (Championship Auto Racing Teams, Inc.) host races for specialty vehicles. And, kids from 5 to 15 years old can race in go-karts and 150-cc quarter midgets.

NASCAR superstar Darrell Waltrip gained winning experience with the ASA. Mark Martin and Rusty Wallace also won at ASA races.

CHAPTER TWO

STOCK, BUT NOT

In the early days of stock car racing, drivers simply showed up on race day. They drove Chevrolets, Dodges, Pontiacs, and Fords. They also drove Hudsons, Kaisers, Lincolns, Mercurys, Oldmobiles, Cadillacs, and Studebakers.

A few drivers bought their stock cars just a few days before a race or borrowed their "rides" from rich owners. Some drivers towed their racing vehicles behind the family sedans. Others drove the family sedans to—and in—the race. Wrecking the cars in a race often meant a long walk home.

BUILT FOR SPEED

In the early 1950s, Bill France, Sr., helped to bring carmakers into the sport. They offered tips, developed racing parts, and improved handling. But in the mid-1950s, the Automobile Manufacturers Association (AMA) banned members from helping racers. The ban lasted until 1962.

Today, NASCAR makes deals with manufacturers to decide which cars can enter its races. In 2003, NASCAR allowed only one vehicle model from four American manufacturers:

• Taurus from Ford
• Monte Carlo from Chevrolet
• Grand Prix from Pontiac
• Intrepid from Dodge

The difference between the normal "street" model that anyone can buy today and a NASCAR stock car is like the difference between a calico kitten and a cheetah. They share similar characteristics, but they're two very different animals. For a NASCAR racing car to run fast, its team builds an engine that doesn't just purr. It roars!

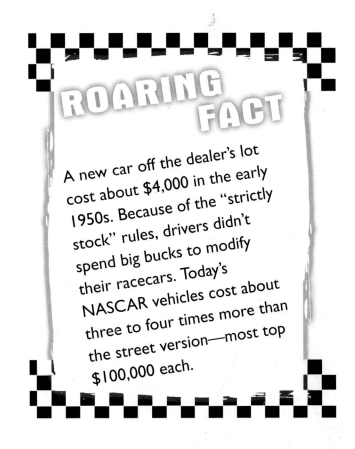

ROARING FACT

A new car off the dealer's lot cost about $4,000 in the early 1950s. Because of the "strictly stock" rules, drivers didn't spend big bucks to modify their racecars. Today's NASCAR vehicles cost about three to four times more than the street version—most top $100,000 each.

◄ *Today's stock cars are not as "stock" as the early models. Dodge recently returned to NASCAR with the Intrepid model.*

THE CORE TEAM MEMBERS

Owner – Owns the vehicle; may provide financial support for team

Driver – Drives the vehicle; he or she usually works on it, too

Crew chief – Coaches the team; makes the big decisions

Car chief – Sets up the car before it's hauled to the track; decides who works on the cars

Fabricator – Creates the sheet metal body of a stock car, using the manufacturer's model

Engineer – Figures out how to improve the car's performance

Mechanic – Builds or fixes the moving parts in a car

Spotter – Reports race opportunities or dangers, including weather, and makes deals with other teams for drafting partners

Pit crew – Prepares and maintains the car at the racetrack

OTHER EXPERTS:

Aerodynamicist – Studies the car's behavior in air

Tire specialist – Checks tire performance and plans tire use for each race

Body specialist – Designs the sleek car body for the best aerodynamics and safety within NASCAR's rules

Team scorer – Calculates the driver's NASCAR points and sets goals to win the championship

Trainer – Helps drivers and pit crew members lift weights and work out regularly

Each driver works with a large team of highly skilled people. ▶
Some team members work behind the scenes in the garage or on pit road. Other important people also include the families, sponsors, and publicity staff.

LOSING WEIGHT

A team of specialists builds each car piece by piece. They **modify**, or change, many parts to boost performance. The teams tweak and tune the V-8 engines to deliver about 700 horsepower. But every change must follow NASCAR rules.

A lighter car moves faster. To make the race fair, NASCAR rules say all the cars must weigh at least 3,400 pounds (1,542 kg) ready to race with fuel, oil, and other liquids. The seated driver adds another 200 pounds (90.7 kg). If he or she is lighter than that, the team puts special weights in the car.

The team also removes any extra weight until the car is down to 3,400 pounds (1,542 kg). The door and trunk hinges disappear. The driver hops in through the side window instead. Most headlights are just fancy stickers, not working lights. Also unlike normal cars, a stock car has only one seat and no stereo.

ALIKE BUT DIFFERENT

Some racing car parts look like "street" versions. Most racing parts feature special changes to help the racing car handle better or keep the driver safe.

A normal car and a stock car both use **gauges** in the dashboard, but different kinds. A stock car doesn't have a gas gauge (the pit crew figures out when to add gas). It also has no speedometer (the driver just goes as fast as possible). Instead, gauges in stock cars measure water temperature, oil pressure, and fuel pressure.

A car on the dealer's lot usually comes with an automatic **transmission** and front-wheel drive. Stock cars use a shifting lever for the manual transmission and rear-wheel drive.

ROARING FACT

NASCAR's (Almost) All-American Sport

Since it began, NASCAR has handed the checkered flag to only one foreign car at a major race—a Jaguar won in Linden, N.J., in 1954. The first Toyota will enter a NASCAR Craftsman Truck Series in 2004. Maybe a Camry will race in the Nextel by 2007!

Drivers check gauges in their cars to avoid engine trouble. Extra safety gear inside the cab protects the drivers, too.

SAFETY INSIDE AND OUT

Manufacturers build their cars with many safety features. A racing team builds its car that way, too. The **chassis**, or frame, uses thick tubing in the car's middle. It forms the roll cage guarding the driver and holds the seat.

The seat hugs the driver around the ribs and shoulders. At the top of the seat, a boxy padded pillar keeps the driver's head from jerking around in a crash. A padded five-point harness holds the driver in place, like the seat belt in a baby's car seat.

NO BREAKABLE GLASS

Glass windows break too easily for a racecar. Lexan, a clear bullet-proof material, fits into the car's windshield frame. Lexan won't shatter, but it scratches very easily. Layers of clear film stretched over the windshield protect the surface from sand and grit. During the race, the pit crew strips off each dirty layer.

Lexan in goggles or a helmet visor also protects the driver's eyes. Every NASCAR driver must wear a helmet. Most use a full-face model that covers the head and guards the mouth and chin. All helmets have a hard shell, a foam core, and a fire-retardant lining specially fitted to the driver's head.

Instead of a glass driver's side window, the team puts in a strong net. Heavy-duty webbing keeps the driver's arms tucked in and **debris** out, if the car crashes. The netting releases easily to let the driver escape.

In 2001, NASCAR changed its rules about restraint systems. Now all NASCAR vehicles must use head-and-neck restraint systems. The approved HANS (head-and-neck system) or Hutchen's device uses a fitted collar secured to the helmet with tethers to prevent the driver's head from slamming around in a crash.

NONSTOP FIRE SAFETY

NASCAR sets strict rules to reduce fire risks. A firewall between the engine and the cab guards the driver from heat and flames. Drivers wear fire-retardant suits, gloves, socks, and shoes. Pit crews also wear fire-retardant suits. The driver and crew keep fire extinguishers handy, too.

A specially designed fuel cell, or gas tank, in each racing car helps prevent fires, too. This rubber-coated metal box sits at the rear of the vehicle. Inside the shell, a fire-resistant plastic liner filled with foam keeps the car's 110-octane gasoline from sloshing. The foam also reduces the risk of an explosion.

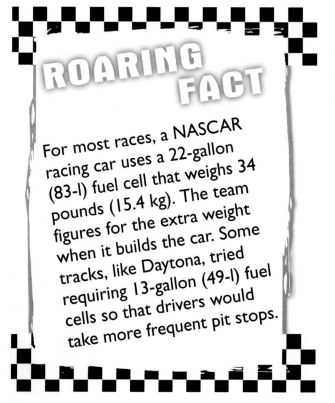

ROARING FACT

For most races, a NASCAR racing car uses a 22-gallon (83-l) fuel cell that weighs 34 pounds (15.4 kg). The team figures for the extra weight when it builds the car. Some tracks, like Daytona, tried requiring 13-gallon (49-l) fuel cells so that drivers would take more frequent pit stops.

The pit crew wears fire-retardant suits, shoes, and gloves. Safety rules!

BALDER AND FATTER

A racing car tire looks balder and fatter than a normal car tire. These smooth **slicks** run quickly on dry pavement. Without tread, slicks can slip and slide on a wet track. NASCAR halts races during rain.

Normal tires can't handle high speeds for long distances. Tires heat and expand then. Inside each NASCAR racing tire, a rubber lining holds special air called **nitrogen**. Nitrogen doesn't damage the tire when it's hot like regular air can do.

The rubber lining also keeps the tire full if the outside tire has a tear or hole. The driver stays in control. But a leak in the inner lining spells trouble. An "equalized" tire has the same air pressure on the inside lining and outside tire. Most people call that *a flat* tire.

In 2003, all Winston Cup cars used Goodyear Racing Eagle tires. A team can easily wear out a dozen or more sets in one race. Each tire costs about $350. Work the math: each team spends more than $16,800 on slicks for one event. Cha-ching!

ROARING FACT

Pure Oil Company made the first stock car racing tire in 1952. Until then, drivers used street tires…and a lot of them. Street tires wore quickly. Until 1965, drivers often built trap doors in the floorboard to check the right front tire, which wore the fastest.

CHAPTER THREE

AIR POWER

A car's behavior in air, called **aerodynamics**, affects the driver's safety as well as the vehicle's performance.

Airflow works a bit like a knife in butter. The thin part of the blade slices best because the fine edge creates very little drag, or resistance. Pushing the wide, flat side into the butter takes more effort. The broad surface area of the knife creates more drag. Engineers try to reduce or remove extra surface areas on cars that plow air. That's one reason why stock cars do not use wing mirrors like normal cars do—they're a real drag.

AIR CONTROLLERS

Air flowing under the car at high speeds can lift the entire vehicle up, flipping it over. Each NASCAR racing car uses an air dam just a few inches off the pavement to block much of the risky air. Rocker skirts along the sides help, too.

Roof flaps became standard in 1994. These devices sit inside pockets near the rear window. The whirling air from a fast spin-out sucks the pockets open. The flaps pop up and cut off the lifting airflow to keep the car on the ground.

Another device simply changes the airflow direction. The angled **spoiler** on the trunk catches air and pulls it down. This airflow presses the car's rear onto the track, adding control to the rear-wheel drive system at high speeds.

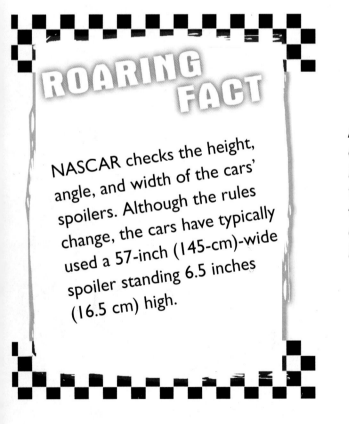

ROARING FACT

NASCAR checks the height, angle, and width of the cars' spoilers. Although the rules change, the cars have typically used a 57-inch (145-cm)-wide spoiler standing 6.5 inches (16.5 cm) high.

Many NASCAR rules focus on safety to avoid crashes like this one. Of course, wrecks still happen. Thanks to better equipment, drivers often walk away from incredibly mangled vehicles. ▶

SAFER, MAYBE

Sometimes a safety device causes trouble, too. In 1988, after Bobby Allison crashed into the grandstand fence at 210 miles (338 km) per hour, NASCAR decided to reduce superspeedway speeds.

Now at Daytona and Talladega superspeedways, each NASCAR racing car must use a square **restrictor plate** where air comes into the engine. This lowers the engine's top speed by about 10 miles (16 km) per hour.

Restrictor plates work so well that all the engines perform almost equally. Nobody pulls ahead of the pack before a line of cars catches up. One mistake in the tight pack sends several cars spinning and crashing.

SHARING AIR

If restrictor plates make engines alike, how does one racer make it to the front? The answer is still about airflow. At superspeedways, drivers use aerodynamics when 43 cars shake up the air at a NASCAR race. If one knife blade slices the butter, then 42 blades behind it will try to follow the same cut.

A two-car **drafting** team gains even more speed than the full line. The second car noses up about a half-car length behind the first car. The second car sucks up the first car's drag. The first car gains speed. At the same time, the first car slices away air for the second car. The second car also gains speed. Drafting helps both cars go faster than either could go alone.

Of course, both cars can't win. Drafting teams form and break away throughout a race. A partnership can last a few laps or even a few seconds—at 190 miles (306 km) per hour, aerodynamics work fast!

ROARING FACT

Seven-time NASCAR champion Dale Earnhardt was the master drafter. Almost as if he could see air, he used airflow from other cars to push and pull his #3 car to victory. "The Intimidator" died in a crash at the 2001 Daytona 500 race.

TRACKING THE TRACKS

As drivers gain experience, they learn each track's secrets. No two courses feel the same. Some use concrete tracks. Others use asphalt. Some follow an oval shape. Others look more like a "D" or an egg.

Wandering road courses are the hardest for stock car drivers to master. Hinting of the old moonshine routes, the courses twist and turn on mostly flat tracks.

A superspeedway like the Daytona International Speedway features long straightaways and banked, or steep, corners. Each banked corner at Daytona measures 31 degrees, which is steeper than some roofs. Banked corners allow the cars to stay on the track at high speeds. Drivers must handle them with care. Most accidents occur in the corners.

ROARING FACT

Aerodynamics comes from the Greek words *aerios*, meaning air, and *dynamis*, meaning power.

DAYTONA INTERNATIONAL SPEEDWAY *World Center of Racing*

When Bill France, Sr., started NASCAR in Daytona Beach, Florida, he also dreamed of building a track there. He helped shape one of the most famous racetracks in the world, the Daytona International Speedway. It opened in 1959.

Today, a sell-out crowd fills the 110,500 seats every February for the Daytona 500, kicking off the NASCAR Cup racing season.

Called the "World Center of Racing," the Daytona International Speedway hosts more types of racing—from stock cars to superbikes—than any other racing venue.

Daytona International Speedway

Length: 2.5 miles (4 km)

Shape: Tri-oval (like a "D")

Infield quirk: The 44-acre (17.8-ha) Lake Lloyd formed when tractors dug soil to build the 31° banked corners

First Winner of Daytona 500: Lee Petty

Most Wins at Daytona 500: Lee Petty's son, Richard – 7 victories between 1964-1981

Qualifying Record: Bill Elliot – 210.364 mph [338.539 kph] (42.783 seconds) on February 9, 1987

Race Record (500 miles): Buddy Baker – 177.602 mph (285.815 kph) on February 17, 1980

Top Speeds: 220 mph (354 kph) on the back straight

Daytona International Speedway features very steep corners.

TRACK NICKNAMES

The unique NASCAR tracks often earn nicknames:

Bristol Motor Speedway – Bristol, Tennessee
"The World's Fastest Half Mile"
.533 mile (.857 km)

Dover International Speedway – Dover, Delaware
"The Monster Mile"
1 mile (1.6 km)

Darlington Raceway – Darlington, South Carolina
"The Track Too Tough to Tame"
1.366 miles (2.198 km)

Strong fences and high barriers protect fans from flying parts. Thick concrete walls keep the cars away from the fans. Someday, "soft walls" made of crushable material may help drivers walk away from today's dangerous wall crashes.

CHAPTER FOUR

HEADED FOR VICTORY LANE

Racing takes hard work. No free-riders! Drivers blend patience and guts with sharp eyes, strong muscles, and quick reflexes.

Drivers work out to build **stamina**. Their bodies must handle 500 miles (805 km), or about 3.5 hours, at top speeds on tracks that easily reach 120°F (48.9°C). Inside the car, temperatures can climb another 50 degrees. They drink plenty of water and never take potty breaks—now that's awesome!

BRAIN POWER

Driving fast requires thinking fast. Smart drivers study how each racer handles corners, drafting, and other strategic moves. Many team members now complete college degrees in engineering, aeronautics, or other related fields. Owners hire educated drivers who understand engines and can work on cars.

Building a NASCAR Team costs millions of dollars. Then teams spend more than $150,000 on each race, not including salaries. Some of the money comes from winning the "purse," or the official prize. Drivers share their earnings with the team and owners.

More money comes from sponsors. They pay to stick their logos on the car, the trailer, the team racing suits—nearly any place that fans or TV cameras might see. The driver says the sponsor's name during every media interview, too. Speaking well in front of a camera attracts bigger and better sponsors—and more team funds.

ROARING FACT

In 1949, NASCAR champion Red Byron earned $5,800. In 1985, Darrell Waltrip became the first NASCAR driver to claim over one million—$1,318,735.

Michael Waltrip celebrates his second victory at the NASCAR Winston Cup Daytona 500, February 16, 2003.

RACING FOR POINTS

Drivers compete for the national championship to earn even more money. Using a complex system, NASCAR awards points to drivers after each event during the season.

The point system works the same way at every track for every race. Racing at the shortest track, .526-mile (.846-km) Martinsville Speedway in Virginia, is just as important as the longest track, 2.66-mile (4.28-km) Talledega Superspeedway in Alabama.

The winner receives 175 points. Then each car crossing the finish line receives fewer points than the one ahead of it. Drivers also earn bonus points for leading a lap and for leading the most laps.

The driver with the most points when the season ends in November takes the championship—and a lot of money.

ROARING FACT

Jeff Gordon was the first driver to exceed 5,000 points in one year (5,143) in 1998. His team finished with more than $8 million in winnings. In contrast, 500 ARCA drivers compete for prizes totaling just under $4 million.

CHAPTER FIVE

LIFE ON THE ROAD

The speedway life looks fun and exciting. Sometimes it is. For drivers and their teams, racing also takes a lot of time away from home. They spend most of their time working on the car or traveling to the next racetrack.

The team eats meals and takes breaks in the hauler truck. Like a garage on wheels, this semi-trailer carries two racecars, spare parts, and tools.

PRACTICE PAYS OFF

During the week, the pit crew practices. NASCAR allows only seven team members on pit road at one time in a race, and each person has one job to do—very quickly.

When the driver pulls into the pit box at the race, the pit crew pounces on the car. The gas man hoists an 80-pound (36.3-kg) dump can up to the fuel cell tube. He pours 11 gallons (41.6 l) of gasoline into the tube, usually twice.

At the same time, the catch-can is plugged into the tank's overflow tube. The team measures the extra gas in the catch-can to plan for its next pit stop.

The fueling happens while the jackman raises the car for the tire guys to change the tires. Using air-powered tools and fancy footwork, the pit crew quickly adjusts the **suspension** and tweaks the engine, too. The team sends the car back on the track in about 18 seconds.

The annual Union 76 World Championship Pit Crew Competition shows the talents of the fastest pit crews. These guys train and lift weights to stay in shape for their jobs.

41

Every weekend during the season, the teams battle for a chance to see their car drive down Victory Lane—the track's glory spot. What's a typical weekend like?

Friday - Practice in the morning. Qualifiers, or time trials, in the afternoon give each driver a chance to run alone as fast as possible on the track. The fastest lap time decides who gets the pole position—the inside left of the first row in the racing line-up.

Saturday - More practicing and more qualifying. The fastest 36 cars receive starting places for the race. Drivers practice again during "Happy Hour," the final 60 minutes before NASCAR shuts down the garages for the night.

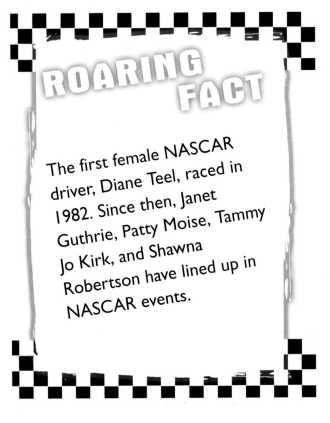

ROARING FACT

The first female NASCAR driver, Diane Teel, raced in 1982. Since then, Janet Guthrie, Patty Moise, Tammy Jo Kirk, and Shawna Robertson have lined up in NASCAR events.

Sunday - Garages open at 6:00 a.m. The cars, tools, and gear move to pit road. Judges inspect cars. NASCAR officials meet with drivers and crew chiefs to talk about the rules and safety. Teams push the cars into place, side by side, in two long lines. Then the announcer yells, "Start your engines!" The cars parade slowly around the track behind the pace car until the judges decide it's time to race. Then the flagman waves the green flag and the battle begins!

Drivers talk with their teams about strategy, car performance, and other drivers. Fans use scanners to hear the chatter.

RACE TALK

Flying around a track, drivers focus on controlling the car. It's noisy. To stay tuned in with their teams, stock car drivers wear headsets and use two-way radios.

The teams use radios. But NASCAR, like most American racing organizations, uses color-coded flags to tell the drivers about the race. One official waves the flags from a platform at the start-finish line where drivers can easily see the colors.

Green: Start

 Yellow: Caution; slow, no passing

 Black: Pull into pit; driver likely broke a rule or has car trouble

White Cross: No scoring for that car until it pulls into pit

White: Last lap

 Yellow/Red Striped: Dangerous track

 Blue/Yellow Striped: Faster cars gaining lap; best to move out of the way

 Red Flag: Stop everything! No racing, no fueling, no repairs in the garage

Black/White Checkered: End of the race

NEED MORE SPEED?

Some fans can't get enough racing action from the grandstands or TV. They need real speed. High-performance or racecar-driving schools around the country put teenagers and adults behind the wheel for a wild ride in the fast lane.

Everything from half-day to three-day or even private lessons are offered, with fees ranging from $450 to more than $5,000.

For most fans, cruising a few museums or the local library does the trick. Many books and magazines cover stock car racing. The Internet also offers many updated web sites.

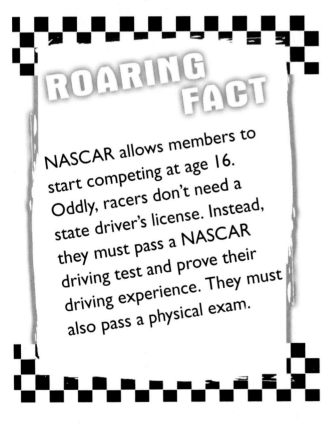

ROARING FACT

NASCAR allows members to start competing at age 16. Oddly, racers don't need a state driver's license. Instead, they must pass a NASCAR driving test and prove their driving experience. They must also pass a physical exam.

Further Reading

Daytona 500 (NASCAR! series) by Eric Ethan. Gareth Stevens Publishing, 1999.

NASCAR (Game Plan series) by Tom Owens and Diana Star Helmer. Millbrook Press, 2000.

The Official NASCAR Preview and Press Guide 2003. NASCAR/UMI Publications, 2003.

Stock Car Kings (All Aboard Reading series) by Andrew Gutelle. Grosset & Dunlap, 2001.

Tradin' Paint: Raceway Rookies and Royalty by Terry Bisson. Scholastic, Inc., 2001.

Web Sites

American Speed Association
http://www.asaracing.com

Auto Racing Schools Online Resource
http://www.racingschools.com

Automobile Racing Clubs of America (ARCA)
http://www.arcaracing.com

Official Web site of the National Association for
Stock Car Auto Racing
http://www.nascar.com

Go Racing - Results Online
http://www.goracing.com

Jayski / That's Racin' Online Resource
http://jayski.thatsracin.com

Glossary

aerodynamics (ahr oh dih NAM iks) — in racing, the effect of air on a moving car

chassis (CHASS ee) — the frame that supports the body of a vehicle

debris (dah BREE) — broken parts or garbage

disqualify (dis KWOL ah FIY) — to take away the privilege to participate in or win contests; to remove from competition

drafting (DRAFT ing) — in racing, to use the flow of air to gain speed

gauges (GAY jez) — devices that show standard measurements, such as speed in miles or kilometers per hour

modify (MOD ah fih) — to change somewhat from the original form

nitrogen (NIH trah jen) — a colorless, odorless gas

restrictor plate (ri STRIK tur PLAYT) — a small, aluminum plate installed in a racecar engine to reduce air flowing to the carburetor; less air means less horsepower for less speed

sanction (SANGK shun) — to approve or to allow; to make rules

slicks (SLIKS) — wide racing tires with smooth surfaces for use on dry asphalt or cement race tracks

spoiler (SPOY lur) — a fin or blade device that breaks up the air flowing over a car to decrease lift and increase traction at high speeds

stamina (STAM ah nah) — strength and power to keep going, to continue

suspension (sah SPEN shun) — in vehicles, the system of shock absorbers, springs, and other parts between the wheel and chassis designed to create a smooth ride and better control

transmission (trans MISH un) — in vehicles, the unit of gears that allows the engine's power to move the wheels

Index

aerodynamics   27, 30
air dam   28
Automobile Manufacturers
    Association (AMA)   16
American Speed Association
    (ASA)   13
Automobile Racing Clubs
    of America (ARCA)   13, 38
chassis   22
Daytona International Speedway
    31, 32, 34
drafting   30, 36
France, Bill, Junior   12
France, Bill, Senior   6, 8, 13,
    16, 32
fuel cell   24, 40
gauges   20

Lexan   22
moonshine   6, 31
National Association for Stock
    Car Auto Racing (NASCAR)
    6, 8, 11, 12, 13, 16, 17, 19, 22,
    24, 26, 28, 29, 30, 34, 38, 40,
    42, 43, 44
nitrogen   26
pit crew   22, 24, 40
racecar driving schools   44
restrictor plate   29, 30
roof flaps   28
slicks   26
spoiler   28
sponsors   10, 36
stamina   35
transmission   20

About The Author

Tracy Nelson Maurer specializes in nonfiction and business writing. Her most recently published children's books include the RadSports series, also from Rourke Publishing LLC. Tracy lives with her husband Mike and two children near Minneapolis, Minnesota.